First published 2022

(c) 2022 Dominic Salles

All rights reserved. The right of Dominic Salles to be identified as the Author of this work has been asserted by them in accordance with the Copyright, Designs and Patents Act 1988. No part of this work may be reproduced, stored in a retrieval system, transmitted in any form or by any means, electronical, mechanical, photocopying, recording, or otherwise, without the prior permission of the Author.

Dominic Salles still lives in Swindon, with his workaholic wife Deirdre. His jiu-jitsu-loving ex-engineer son, Harry, has moved to Shoreditch and lives on the site of Shakespeare's first theatre. Destiny. For those of you who remember Bob, he is now an ex-dog.

His daughter Jess is educating students in Wales because, now Brexit is done, Brussels isn't stepping in to help the Welsh any more. She is learning to surf. He spent three months in Andorra this year, learning to snowboard. He is not as cool as he thinks.

His sister Jacey is famous for her Spanish accent, on your TV screens, and is also filming in Wales. She would be hilarious in her own YouTube channel. His 2006 Prius has just died and been rein*car*nated (who writes these puns?) as a 2019 Prius.

His YouTube channel, Mr Salles Teaches English, has reached 100,00o subscribers, about which he is childishly excited. 30% of his viewers said they improved by at least 3 grades in 2022.

Other Grade 9 Guides by Mr Salles

Language

The Mr Salles Guide to **100% at AQA GCSE English Language**
The Mr Salles Guide to **Awesome Story Writing**
The Mr Salles Quick Guide to **Awesome Description**
The Mr Salles **Ultimate Guide to Description**
The Mr Salles Quick Guide to **Grammar, Punctuation and Spelling**
The Mr Salles Ultimate Guide to **Persuasive Writing**
The Mr Salles Guide to **100% in AQA GCSE English Language Paper 1 Question 2**

Literature

The Mr Salles Guide to **GCSE English Literature**
Study Guide Mr Salles Analyses **Jekyll and Hyde**
The Mr Salles Ultimate Guide to **Macbeth**
The Mr Salles Guide to **An Inspector Calls**
The Mr Salles Ultimate Guide to **A Christmas Carol**
The Mr Salles Ultimate Guide to **Romeo and Juliet**
Mr Salles **Power and Conflict** Top Grade Essay Guide (AQA Anthology): 11 Grade 9 Exam Essays!

Introduction

This guide is built round such a simple idea, that I'm shocked I never thought of it before.

The best way to understand exam answers is to read exam answers!

For each question, I want my readers to have a huge range of exam answers to past questions. You will get at 24 answers, all marked to show you the full range of the mark scheme.

And I also give you my commentary for each one as to why the marks were awarded.

In real life, most of these answers would be full of spelling and punctuation errors, and still get the marks. Students who are very bad writers can still get good grades. But I've made sure that the spelling and punctuation is correct, so you can focus precisely on the exam skills of each question.

I've also rewritten each answer so that they actually make sense, and so that the students who wrote them wouldn't recognise them. I've changed most words, so 'green' becomes 'red', 'he' becomes 'she', 'fast' becomes 'quick' etc. It means the skills, sentences, detail and type of vocabulary is exactly the same as the actual students used, while nearly all the individual words are changed.

How to Use This Guide

All the answers are based on actual exam papers, which you can download from the AQA website. For copyright reasons, I can't give you the actual quotations from the exam paper. But I have rewritten these so that it will be easy for you to match up each answer with the right exam paper.

However, the guide will work brilliantly on its own, without the exam papers if you prefer.

1. Any time you sit any exam question, put your answer alongside this guide. Ask yourself, "which answer in the guide looks most like my answer?"

2. This will give you a very good guide as to what mark your answer would get.

3. Then read my commentary underneath.

4. This will tell you the sorts of things you are probably doing wrong.

5. Now, read the answers that scored more than this. Build up an idea of what gets more marks. This is even more valuable than my examiner's comments. But, you should read those too, because they teach you everything you need to know.

6. Now, write your answer again, without looking at the guide. This is the **only** way for you to work out if your exam skills are improving. If you answer a **different** question from a different paper, you won't know if you miss marks because you haven't understood the text properly, or because of a lack of exam technique.

7. **After** you have practised exam technique a couple of times, then you should try a **new** exam paper. This will measure how much improvement you have actually made, and tell you what mark you are likely to get if you took the GCSE now.

Introduction to Question 3

This is a 'new' question, which had never appeared in any exam before 2017.

Teachers have always found this a puzzling one – they haven't studied the structure of extracts like this for A level or for their degree.

AQA is equally puzzled by it, which is why they give it only 8 marks. They have found students write a lot more for question 3 than question 2, even though question 2 is also worth the same 8 marks.

This is a problem I will try to cure.

The second problem AQA hadn't anticipated is with the wording of the question which suggests you should look at 'sentence forms'. This led to students writing gibberish. The examiners now say don't write about sentence forms, you'll only write gibberish. I agree.

Amazingly, there is a stunningly simple way to answer this question and get 100%. It is obviously called the Mr Salles Method, and you'll meet it in just a minute.

Mark Scheme

The mark scheme tries to grade this in all sorts of abstract ways.

a) **Perceptive, detailed analysis 7-8 marks**
b) **Clear, relevant explanation 5-6 marks**
c) **Some understanding and comment 3-4 marks**
d) **Simple, limited comment 1-2 marks**
e) **(Note this is exactly the same as for question 2)**

What's the difference between simple and some? Between understand and explanation? Between clear and perceptive? You get the idea. Put two English teachers together, and they will probably disagree. The marks scheme is nowhere near as helpful as AQA would have us believe.

In fact, trained AQA examiners are allowed to give wildly different marks before their marking is checked. 8 marks out of 40 is the tolerable limit. So, a 20% difference. In other words, a chief examiner might give a question 2 response 6 marks, while two normal examiners might give it 5 and 7 respectively. All these marks would be considered ok!

That's because the wording of the mark scheme is vague, abstract, and open to interpretation.

The mark scheme makes the question suddenly seem pretty difficult. It isn't.

The Mr Salles Method

After analysing over 100 exam answers which have been marked by senior examiners, I have worked out a method for getting the mark right in every single one.

I know this sounds unlikely, but it is true.

1. **Write about the first focus. This will be whatever the first paragraph is about.**
2. **Write about 6 of the other paragraphs, as changes of focus.**
3. **With each focus and change of focus, explain how that affects what we think, feel or predict.**
4. **Write about the last paragraph, and its change of focus.**
5. **That will give you 8 changes of focus, 8 explanations of the effect on the reader, and 8 marks.**

   Why don't the examiners publish that as the mark scheme?

1. Ofqual, who oversee all the exam boards in the UK, might not let them.

2. AQA, like all exam boards, want to pretend that their exams test skills that are 100% relevant to English, rather than simply random exam technique. If you need proof that AQA know that the mark scheme is a problem, here it is. This is from an email AQA sent me just today:

   "GCSE English Language: Mark scheme guidance and application – This free course is available virtually from 5th September – 31st December."

   That's right, the mark scheme is so confusing that trained English teachers, who also have degrees in English and have taught hundreds or thousands of students, can't agree what it means! And the course lasts 2 hours. Forgive me, but WTF?

3. If AQA made the marks scheme really easy to understand, too many average students would start to score many more marks, so it would be really difficult to work out sensible grade boundaries.

4. For example, Paper 1 is worth 80 marks. Examiners are allowed to differ by 16 marks. 10 marks is often the difference between grades now. So, already, there is a high probability that a student can be given a wrong grade. Now, if the mark scheme helps average students get more marks, a massive problem happens. Imagine that the difference between grades is only 5 marks. 16 marks is now worth 3 grades. What are the chances that a student will be given the wrong grade for the paper? Huge.

5. Am I really saying that AQA can't afford for lots of students to start doing well in the exam? Yes, that's exactly what I am saying.

When You Read the Student Exam Answers

You will notice that I lay out each answer as numbered bullet points.

You don't have to write your exam answers this way. However, if you did, you would help the examiner. They would easily be able to see how many quotations you are using, how many points you are making, and how many explanations you are giving about what we think, feel or predict.

But it will also make **your** task easier. You will write less, and still get the marks. You will know when you have written a full mark answer. This is especially useful in your exam practice and revision.

Many of you will find that you can write more than 8 of these points in 10 minutes. That's fine – sometimes you might write a point which doesn't score, so having more than 8 is a good insurance.

But never go over your time limit! (You have 12 minutes to read the question and the extract and write your answer).

Adapted From Language Paper 1 November 2020

Question 3

You now need to think about the **whole** of the source.

How has the writer structured the text to interest you as a reader?

You could write about:

- what the writer focuses your attention on at the beginning of the source
- how and why the writer changes this focus as the source develops
- any other structural features that interest you.

[8 marks]

Response 1

1. At the beginning of the source, the writer focuses our attention on the "eerie hound" *so we want to uncover the mystery of who she is.*

2. The writer also deliberately varies our focus by describing the trees and events in the "strange field". *This variety stops the writing being boring.*

3. *Another way to stop the writing being boring* is by using a variety of sentence lengths.

2 marks

My Commentary

a. The student explains something about the change of focus in two parts of the text, in points 1 and 2.
b. Although sentence lengths or sentence types are a choice the writer has made about structure, they do not get any marks. This is because question 3 is always interested in the *change of focus*, and that's it.
c. **Simple, limited comment 1-2 marks**

Response 2

1. The beginning of the extract focuses on the fact that this is Robert's "first morning" in the house.

2. Then we focus on how she saw the "eerie hound".

3. Next the focus returns to Robert.

4. *These changes of focus are deliberate. They limit what we discover about the mysterious child.*

5. *This prompts us to want to discover more about this child.*

6. The writer also varies the length of paragraphs which affects the pace at which they are read. This creates suspense or excitement.

7. The writer places a two line paragraph in the middle of the extract, which focuses on the "eerie hound".

8. *This creates a sense of ambiguity, making us wonder who the child is and how she has appeared in the field.*

3 marks

My Commentary

a. The student has made 8 points, but gets only 3 marks. What is going on?
b. Points 1, 2 and 3 only tell us (correctly) about 3 changes of focus. But they get no marks, because they have no explanation of the effect of these on the reader.
c. A combined effect of points 1-3 is given in point 4, so it gets a mark.
d. Every writer uses paragraphs of different lengths, for all sorts of different effects. So commenting on this never earns any marks. Write about a specific change of focus, instead.
e. Point 7 correctly points out a change of focus, but gives no effect of this on the reader, so it doesn't get a mark.
f. In my italics you can see the three times that the student has tried to explain the effect of three particular changes of focus in points 4, 5 and 8.
g. It's the italics which earns the marks.
h. **Some understanding and comment 3-4 marks**

Response 3

1. At the beginning the writer focuses on Robert's family and how his son is playing with *"ants and beetles and worms"*.

2. Then the focus shifts to the animal like field with its tree "choked" with ivy.

3. The beginning of the text also focuses on the "eerie hound" who has entered the field.

4. Then the writer focuses on Robert's feelings and *how "dispirited" he is by the tasks ahead of her.*

5. At the end of the text the writer focus on the "eerie hound" *to develop our understanding of her.*

6. For example, focusing on when Robert had "noticed the dog's anxious expression" *makes us wonder why it appears so scared and anxious.*

7. *This focus also makes us wonder how it came to be in the field.*

4 marks

My Commentary

a. The student has listed 7 changes of focus. Why don't they get 7 marks?
b. Points 1-3 don't explain any effects on the reader.
c. In italics, the student has explained the effects of these changes of focus.
d. There are 4 explanations of the effects on the reader, so there are 4 marks.
e. **Some understanding and comment 3-4 marks**

Response 4

1. The writer begins by focusing on the fact that Robert is meeting the "eerie" dog for the first time.

2. The writer withholds information about what the dog is doing, or where it has come from, *which creates a problem for the reader to try to solve.*

3. The focus changes to the field itself being mysterious, with descriptions suggesting the field might be dangerous. *This creates tension, where we wonder whether Robert's own children will be in danger.*

4. The extract ends with a cliff hanger of the unexplained disappearance of the eerie hound. *This invites us to predict how the disappearance is possible.*

5. *This creates a sense of mystery.*

6. *This links back to the sense of mystery created at the start of the extract, where we wondered what mystery was hidden in the overgrown field.*

5 marks

My Commentary

a. Point 1 has no explanation, so doesn't score any marks.

b. There are 5 explanations of the effects of the changes of focus.
c. Point 5 also explains how the structure of the text is circular (referring back to something at the start). Examiners literally love this idea, and go to great lengths every year to make sure that the extract does have a circular structure! So this is a point you will be able to make practically any year you sit the exam.
d. **Clear, relevant explanation 5-6 marks**

Response 5

1. At the beginning, the writer focuses on the phrase "eerie hound". *This invites us to wonder what the dog is doing, how it entered the field, and why it came.*

2. The next paragraph focuses on descriptions of the house, where the "*window was stained glass in parts*". *This invites us to wonder about what sort of house this is.*

3. Then the focus changes to a description of the field *in order to give us a clearer picture of where the family live.*

4. The writer also focuses on Robert's children in the field, as "he had carried out a brief assessment of the strange field." *This deliberately refers back to the mystery of the eerie hound introduced at the beginning.*

5. *Focusing on Robert's assessment also makes us wonder how the hound got there without Robert noticing it arrive.*

6. The next change of focus is when *"Lara appeared to ignore this hound". We wonder if Lara is simply too engrossed in her play to notice the eerie hound.*

7. *We also wonder whether in fact this dog is a ghost only Robert can see.*

8. The focus at the end is also on this mystery, when "the giant hound was nowhere to be seen". *We wonder if the dog was real or just a product of his imagination, caused by the "strange" environment of the field.*

6 marks

My Commentary

a. There are 8 explanations for the change of focus.
b. Point 2 looks like it gives us a clear effect on the reader, to make us wonder. But this is very general – even better if this were specific – 'makes us wonder about the age of the house', or 'whether the house had once been part of a church'. So, it is really 0.5 of a mark (which remember the examiner can't award).
c. Point 3 is even more general. Every description gives us a picture. If the student had written 'gives us a picture of the children appearing happy to contrast with the

anxiety of the eerie hound', then we would have a specific effect, and get the mark. So, point 3 gets no marks.
d. The examiner can't give 6.5 marks, so they have to round up, or round down. Their two choices are to decide whether the answer is a **Perceptive, detailed analysis 7-8 marks** or a **Clear, relevant explanation 5-6 marks.** The last 3 points are definitely perceptive. But the examiner decided that the full answer is not detailed enough, and so it is rounded down to 6 marks.
e. How do you work out what detail is? It is a change of focus. There are 6 changes of focus in the answer, so there are only 6 marks.

Response 6

1. The writer begins with a mystery, focusing on the "eerie hound", but withholding what it is doing in the field *so that we are intrigued.*

2. The change of focus to describe the field and the house *makes us keep wondering about the mysterious dog.*

3. The focus on the *"malformed oak"* which *"sent twisting shadow over the struggling plants it caged" adds to this mystery through the detail of the shadows.* Similar elements of mystery occur throughout the text.

4. For example, the paragraph describing the field ends with a focus on a chained gate, *which acts as a cliff hanger.*

5. Next the writer returns to the mystery of the dog from the opening to the text. *Focusing on details about the dog's appearance and doll allows us to picture it clearly.*

6. This deliberate switch of focus back to the dog *forces the reader to try to make connections to explain the mystery of the dog's presence.*

7. *We are invited to wonder how the mysterious field, and the unexplained chained gate, can be linked to the mysterious hound.*

8. The writer also focuses on questions about the dog which Robert asks himself, like "However had she it into the field? ... But how had it climbed the wall?" *This emphasises two mysteries we have to solve.*

7 marks

My Commentary

a) Again, we can see that there are 7 changes of focus, which is why there are 7 marks.
b) There are 8 explanations of the changes of focus, but as we have seen, this is not enough for the marks to be greater than the number of changes of focus.

c) Point 7 is not a change of focus, even though it is a very well explained effect.
d) So, to get 8 marks, you need 8 changes of focus.
e) **Perceptive, detailed analysis 7-8 marks**

Response 7

1. The writer uses a circular structure. The focus at the beginning and the end is on the "eerie hound" *and the mystery of its identity and appearance.*

2. The writer begins by *focusing on Robert's feelings of anxiety*, being "dispirited".

3. This is then contrasted with the focus on his children playing, *which invokes a sense of innocence, to make us anxious about it.*

4. Next she focuses on Robert's "anxieties" of recent days *to increase our unease.*

5. A quick focus on the child then *invites us to make a connection between this anxiety and the appearance of the mysterious girl.*

6. Next the writer focuses on the field, picking on menacing details *which invite us to associate these with the dog which has appeared there.*

7. Focusing on other details like the "malformed oak" of the tree, and the "strangling" ivy *adds to this sinister mood.*

8. The writer focuses on the dog and how it "looked hunched, and this made it appear ready to strike", which *adds to this mood.*

9. The writer tells us the dog quickly glances "as though scared of seeing someone in the upstairs windows watching", and this focus *adds to our sense of unease as we sense its fear, and we know that none of the family are upstairs, so someone else would need to be in the house to overlook the child.*

10. The penultimate focus is a short, two-sentence paragraph. *This abruptness creates tension.*

11. This introduces the final focus into Robert's thoughts, where he plans to approach the dog "slowly", only to find that the hound has disappeared. The final shift reveals this in a one sentence paragraph, *which emphasises the suddenness and surprise of the dog's disappearance.*

8 marks

My Commentary

a) There are 11 points, so do any of them fail to score a mark?

b) Point 1 is an introduction, which summarises the rest of the answer, so does not get a mark on its own.
c) Point 2 is only half an explanation – it needs to be continued – which suggests, which implies, which emphasises etc. So it scores 0.5 marks.
d) Point 10 is not a change of focus. It is also too general – a short paragraph might create excitement, happiness, a fast pace etc. So the point is meaningless. It scores no marks.
e) However, that does leave us with 8.5 marks. As you know, half marks are impossible, so we can only have 8 marks.
f) **Perceptive, detailed analysis 7-8 marks**

Adapted From Language Paper 1 June 2019

Question 3

You now need to think about the **whole** of the **source**.

This text is from the beginning of a short story.

How has the writer structured the text to interest you as a reader?

You could write about:

- what the writer focuses your attention on at the beginning of the source
- how and why the writer changes this focus as the source develops
- any other structural features that interest you.

[8 marks]

   a) **Perceptive, detailed analysis 7-8 marks**
   b) **Clear, relevant explanation 5-6 marks**
   c) **Some understanding and comment 3-4 marks**
   d) **Simple, limited comment 1-2 marks**

Response 1

1. The opening of the source focuses on the old motor truck which is "ancient and discoloured".

2. Later in the source the focus is on the second hand clothes.

3. At the end, the writer focuses on Alicia finding the second hand clothes.

1 mark

My Comment

a. Although the student has correctly identified three focuses in the beginning, middle and end, they have not made any comment on the effect on the reader.
b. So, this means there are three half marks, which as you know can't be awarded. The examiner has to decide whether 1.5 should be rounded up or down. Because there is not even a single explanation of the effect on the reader, it is fair to round down.
c. **Simple, limited comment 1-2 marks**

Response 2

1. The writer has made the text interesting.

2. Firstly, the writer has focused on details of the vehicle, which is "ancient and discoloured." *This implies that the truck has seen better days.*

3. *It also illustrates how Hardstop's family has been on the road for a long time.*

4. Later, the focus is on Hardstop's family who have "emaciated" features, *which invites us to wonder why they are in this state.*

2 marks

My Commentary

a. The student has identified two changes of focus, in points 2 and 4. For each of these they have identified an effect on the reader, so the answer scores 2 marks.
b. Point 1 is not a change of focus, so does not score a mark.
c. Number 3 is not a separate change of focus, so the effect on the reader simply refers back to the point in 2. This is why it does not score an extra mark.
d. **Simple, limited comment 1-2 marks**

Response 3

1. The writer structures the text to interest us. It begins by focusing on the truck, which sets the scene. *These details of the family's lifestyle hook the reader.*

2. Next, the writer introduces the family of three. *This introduces characters, which always interest us in a story.*

3. Then the writer focuses on a harsh conversation where Hardstop abandons Alicia on the road. *This event is designed to shock the reader.*

4. The final focus sends the characters in different directions. *This acts as a kind of cliff hanger, which makes us try to predict what will happen next.*

3 marks

My Commentary

a. The student has written about 4 changes of focus.
b. Then they have explained 4 effects on the reader.
c. We would expect this to score 4 marks.
d. Can you spot which one is a pretend effect?
e. It is point 2. Characters will interest us in any story. The student would need to give a specific thing about the character that the writer focuses on to explain the effect of

this particular character. So point 2 scores only half a mark. As you know, half marks can't be given, so it is rounded down.

f. **Some understanding and comment 3-4 marks**

Response 4

1. The author shifts from focusing on the whole scene into specific details, which entices us.

2. The first paragraph focuses on the appearance of the truck and scene through which it is travelling.

3. Next, the focus changes to the characters in the truck, and their appearance. *This helps us understand their circumstances, and we are intrigued to discover more about them.*

4. Later, the writer focuses on building tension, through a short sentence: "they listened, sitting motionlessly". *This builds tension as the characters try to calculate the cause of the noise. We do the same.*

5. Then a complex sentence *builds our sense of fear about what might happen to Alicia.*

6. This change of focus to Alicia *helps us understand how she and Hardstop react to their situation. We experience it with Alicia.*

7. The asyndetic list "Hardstop was at the wheel: an emaciated, sharp-boned man, hollow-cheeked" *draws us in, and makes us sympathetic to him.*

8. We are drawn in to his malnourished and weak appearance, and want to learn more about his character.

4 marks

My Commentary

a. Although it looks as though the student has written many more than 4 points, with more than 4 explanations for the reader, much of the answer has been wasted.
b. Points 1 and 2 don't score marks, as they don't deal with the effect on the reader.
c. Points 3, 4, 6 and 7 do score marks, because they make a point about the change of focus and explain the effect on the reader.
d. Point 5 gives us an effect on the reader, but the point doesn't work. The student would have to tell us what the focus was in this sentence for the explanation to work.

e. Point 8 explains the effect on the reader, but it is only a developed explanation of the point in 7. To gain an extra mark, the explanation would need to refer to a new change of focus.
f. Consequently, the student is limited to 4 marks.
g. **Some understanding and comment 3-4 marks**

Response 5

1. *We are engaged at the start* by a description of extreme weather.

2. The focus on the power of the weather where "the rains flooded the windscreen", and the "near blackness" *invite us to wonder how the family will cope driving in these conditions.*

3. At the beginning, the focus is on the whole Hardstop family together in the truck, with Hardstop "spreading his legs unthinkingly; his spouse and their child Alicia were squashed together, his daughter with arms ironed flat to her sides, and skinny legs forced tightly into a tiny space."

4. This is then contrasted to Alicia's abandonment, *when she appears diminished.*

5. When she proceeds to "vanish into the darkness, still mute" *we wonder if she will ever be reunited with her family.*

6. *If so, this also makes us wonder whether she will be appreciated by them.*

5 marks

My Commentary

a. Points 1-5 all write about a change of focus.
b. Point 3 tells us the change of focus, but not the effect of this on the reader, so it can only score 0.5 marks.
c. Point 6 gives a further effect on the reader to the change of focus in point 5. So, although 0.5 marks can't be awarded, the examiner adds it to the 0.5 marks from Point 3.
d. This means the answer as a whole is worth 5 marks.
e. **Clear, relevant explanation 5-6 marks**

Response 6

1. The writers starts by building suspense through the description of setting.

2. The narrative unfolds in November, *which we associate with miserable weather and thus a mood of misery, which is reflected in the heavy rain which "battered the cab of the truck".*

3. *Added to this is a sense of eeriness* conveyed by the truck moving slowly, *as though waiting for something to happen.*

4. The middle of the source focuses on short sentences and dialogue. *These create a fast paced rhythm, perhaps to echo the readers heartbeat and sense of tension as we anticipate what might happen next.* This acts as a contrast to the slow pace of the truck.

5. Tension is further conveyed through description of the worsening weather, where "hailing viciously". *We realise Alicia is unsheltered, and missing the protection of her parents, and we are possibly scared for her by the eerie setting.*

6. *We want to know what happens to Alicia* as she is described walking away and vanishing. *This makes us sympathetic towards her.*

7. *Tension is also maintained* with the structural device of a cliff-hanger.

8. Focusing on how Hardstop remains in the comfort of the truck while Alicia is forced to sell flowers in the persistent rain *engenders a feeling of disgust towards him, as we question his motives.*

9. The main impact of the writer's choice of structure *is to create tension.*

6 marks

My Commentary

a. Points 1 and 9 are summary statements, which repeat each other. They don't give any examples of changes of focus, as they are an introduction and a conclusion. They show what the student's argument is, but not the specifics of each step. So, they don't directly contribute to a mark.
b. This leaves points 2-8, which could score 7 marks. So which ones don't score?
c. Point 4 is a structural feature, but it is not really a change of focus – it scores 0.5 marks.
d. Point 7 explains the effect on the reader, but it is not a new change of focus – it refers back to the change of focus in point 6. So, this also scores 0.5 marks.
e. As you know, the examiner can't really score any points with 0.5 marks, but taken together points 4 and 7 are worth one mark.
f. So the total is 6 marks.
g. **Clear, relevant explanation 5-6 marks**

Response 7

1. The focus on the truck and its drive through a "a barren, windswept moor" *creates a sense of mystery.*

2. Next the focus shifts to the truck and Hardstop who "was at the wheel" *which adds to the uneasy atmosphere.*

3. The family is described in contrast to Hardstop *which develops the feeling of mystery and tension.*

4. The focus switches to Hardstop's "cautious driving" *in order to build towards a climax.*

5. The writer switches to dialogue, with Hardstop's question, "What the hell was that?" But he disregards his wife's answer, *which causes us to dislike him.*

6. The focus on Alicia as she begins to move even before Hardstop's dialogue *makes us realise this is probably a regular task for her, and so evokes our sympathy.*

7. Focusing on Alicia's isolation *helps us understand Hardstop's cruelty.*

8. Continuing this for two paragraphs *emphasises the duration of her suffering in the rain and heightens our sympathy.*

9. The focus on Alicia finding the flowers acts *as a kind of resolution.*

10. However, Hardstop's resulting anger surprises us as it prevents this resolution and implies a different kind of climax.

11. Alicia's silence and lack of dialogue at the end *causes us to feel further sympathy as we recognise the unfairness of her situation.*

8 marks

My Commentary

a. We can see from the italics that there are 11 points and 11 effects on the reader. Does this mean that you need to write more than 8 such developed points in order to get 8 marks?
b. No. Point 2 is a pretend point. The student gives no reason why Hardstop driving the truck creates tension. So, this scores 0 marks.
c. Point 3 looks like a well-structured point and explanation, but really it is a pretend point. If characters are different, does that really create mystery or tension? Not necessarily. I am sure you might be different to many of your friends. That doesn't create mystery or tension though, does it? The student would need to give a real example for this to be true here. So, this scores 0 marks.

d. Point 4 is another pretend point. How does any character's caution build towards a climax? It works if the character is in danger, but Hardstop doesn't seem to be in danger. So this scores 0 marks.
e. **Perceptive, detailed analysis 7-8 marks**

Response 8

1. The extract in this source is structured so that the first half is exposition, and the second half is rising action.

2. *The atmosphere in the exposition is passive and gloomy. The characters are subdued in the claustrophobic* setting of the truck which "coughed and spluttered".

3. Next there is a dramatic transition from *the "mute" and anxious family, who now become acrimonious.*

4. This transition is emphasised by the sudden appearance of dialogue, *whose purpose is to shock us, because Hardstop's anger, which appears abusive, is also revealed.*

5. *We become curious to understand the unconventional family.*

6. Whereas the exposition focused on Hardstop, the second half focuses on Alicia. *This builds intrigue, as the two characters are now placed in direct contrast with each other.*

7. Hardstop's authoritarian nature is juxtaposed with Alicia's habit of submission, *which makes us wonder how their relationship will progress. We wonder whether Alicia can escape his authority.*

8. The text therefore ends on a cliff-hanger, *leaving us with uncertainty and tension.*

9. Interestingly, the focus simply glosses over the third character, who is referred to only as "the companion". *This lack of character development also fascinates us. We ask ourselves how the family dynamic works.*

10. *And it makes us wonder about her part in Alicia's future.*

8 marks

My Commentary

a. The opening sentence works as a summary of the whole piece, and shows the examiner that you understand the whole structure. This is an easy way to show that you have evaluated the whole source.
b. In practice, this can be hard to do because of exam pressure. So, the easiest way is to write the rest of your answer first. Make sure you leave two or three lines at the beginning, which you can fill in later with your overall summary. When you have

written your points, it will be easy for you to fill in this gap, as the overall structure will now be obvious to you.
c. That said, on its own, it scores no marks.
d. There are 9 explanations in the remaining 9 points.
e. Points 5 and 10 are excellent explanations, but refer back to earlier changes of focus. They score half a point each.
f. This does mean that there are only 7 changes of focus, where we would expect 8 for full marks. This is where point 1 has helped tip the examiner into deciding that the 8 marks are fair.
g. **Perceptive, detailed analysis 7-8 marks**

Adapted From Language Paper 1 November 2018

Question 3

You now need to think about the **whole** of the source.

This text is from the middle of a short story.

How has the writer structured the text to interest you as a reader?

You could write about:

- what the writer focuses your attention on at the beginning of the source
- how and why the writer changes this focus as the source develops
- any other structural features that interest you.

8 marks

Response 1

1. *The extract interests us* by beginning with a description of the robot *which then suddenly becomes much more dramatic.*

2. The writer has also used a range of complex and short sentences, and some which are incredibly detailed. Having this variety stops readers from becoming bored.

1 mark

My Commentary

a. The student has made one point about the focus, or change of focus, in the extract. This gets one mark.
b. Point two gains no marks. Of course, sentence choice is a choice that the writer is making about structure. But the examiner doesn't care about the types of sentences. They are just interested in the changes of focus in the text.
c. Don't make it harder – it is a very easy question because, guess what, every single paragraph is always a change of focus. They're right there, saying, "easy marks, come get me".

Response 2

1. The writer has structured the extract by starting with the setting then slowly introducing the Robot.

2. The writer focuses on "the uncanny quiet" and then immediately changes the focus in the next sentence to "a thunderclap". *This sudden change in sound helps us imagine the Robot which is going to be described in the next paragraph.*

3. This focus then gives us lots of detail about the Robot *so we can picture it.*

4. Then the focus moves to characters' speech, *so that we can relate to their experience.*

3 marks

My Commentary

a) The student has made 4 points.
b) Point 1 doesn't comment on the effect on the reader, but points 2, 3 and 4 do, so they get one mark each.

Response 3

1. The text begins with a description of the jungle. *This makes it appear both magical and like a setting for a dream,* so "strange songs and the beating of giant wings echoed through the canopy".

2. Next the focus changes to the Robot, which "soared forty feet over the treeline, a massive, malignant deity". *This portrays a vivid image and indicates that the Robot will play a major role in the story.*

3. There is a shift in focus again as the huge Robot begins to chase the two mean. The short sentence, "It's staring straight at us!" *creates tension as we read on to discover if they will survive.*

4. The extract ends *with a happy ending*: "like the Titanic, like Atlantis, the Robot tipped and sank, swallowed by a sea of green". *We are happy and relieved that the men have all survived, and the deadly monster has been killed.*

4 marks

My Commentary

a) The student has identified four changes of focus.
b) For each one, they have explained the effect on the reader.
c) So they gain 4 marks.

Response 4

1. At the beginning of the extract the writer focuses on how the warriors have fought many battles in the past. *This is interesting, because it reveals that the warriors have previously had no fear of the enemies they have fought.*

2. Later the focus switches to a description of the Robot, *which suggests it is fierce and undefeatable.*

3. At the same time, the focus on the robot's immense power and the toughness of its armour *emphasise that the warriors can't capture it or destroy it.*

4. Later the focus switches to the meeting of the warriors and the Robot, so we find out how surprised the warriors are at the speed of movement of this machine. *This suggests it can escape their plan to destroy it.*

5. Towards the end, the focus is on the warriors' desperate attempts to stop the robot, the movement of its body and swinging tail crashing into the trees.

6. At the end of the text we focus on the Robot crashing to the ground as they have completed their mission and destroyed it.

7. The changes of focus from the warriors to the Robot *help us understand the warriors' viewpoint, and then the facts about the robot's real power.*

8. Then the writer focuses on the meeting between the robot and the warriors.

9. The main focus of the narrative is whether the warriors will be able to destroy the immense and powerful robotic monster.

10. Other structural features which interest us is how the robot is presented as an undefeatable force. The writer presents the warriors as brave and determined to defeat the Robot.

5 marks

My Commentary

a. This is a typical answer of how students both gain marks and leave them behind.
b. The good news is that, if you keep making points, enough of them will score marks.
c. It would be great if this student had actually thought about how they were going to gain marks, which is to add an explanation of the effect on the reader for *each* point.
d. You can see how this works in points 1, 2, 3, 4, 7. Sadly, this is a student who writes enough to get full marks, but they have chucked 3 marks away by having rubbish exam technique.

Response 5

1. The beginning of the text focuses on the "green" and "musical" jungle *which creates an atmosphere of peace and calm.*

2. This contrasts with the end of the text, where the focus is on the warriors and their panic before they destroy the Robot.

3. The writer also contrasts the sounds like "song" at the beginning of the text with the ending which has "shrieking". *This causes us to feel fear and anxiety about the power of the Robot.*

4. There is a frequent focus on speech which helps us experience the characters' fears. *This builds tension.*

5. The writer also contrasts Eugene's "hushed" speech with Tarquin's speech where he "ordered". *This creates a feeling of urgency and anxiety and conflict, as the characters disagree about how to act.*

6. Long and complex sentences are used to describe the Robot. *This creates a sense of amazement at the Robot.*

7. The focus on some of the listed characteristics of the robot, like *"two snake-like tentacles" and "the huge swelling carapace of the torso" reveal the characters' sense of shock and create a feeling of anxiety.*

8. In addition, the many long clauses slow down time.

9. In conclusion, the focus on the description of the Robot shows that it is lethal. This increases tension which is contrasted to the slow passage of time produced by the long clauses. *This causes us to feel a sense of panic in us, as we imagine that the warriors will probably die.*

6 marks

My Commentary

a. You know the drill by now. You only get a mark if your point leads to an explanation of the impact on the reader.
b. Here those points are 1, 3, 4, 5, 6 and 9.
c. You can also see that writing about sentence types is not a worthwhile aspect of structure. All you need to do is write about the changes of focus. It ain't hard.
d. As in the previous answer, this student writes enough to gain full marks. If only they had learned the proper exam technique.

Response 6

1. The beginning of the source describes the jungle with "strange song". *This evokes a magical and peaceful place.*

2. We then meet a long descriptive sentence *in order to help us picture the scene.*

3. We are quickly introduced to Tarquin and Eugene. The writer chooses telling details about Eugene, who says "I've fought in the battles of Orwell, of Wuthering Heights, Silas and Marner." *This is to help us deduce that he is an experienced warrior.*

4. Next we learn that he is here "in order to destroy Robot X". *This builds tension, as we are intrigued to discover if this is possible.*

5. Setting the narrative in a jungle also *creates a sense of mystery which invites us to imagine a negative outcome.*

6. The beginning of the extract starts peacefully, with the Robot "one hundred yards away". This is a contrast to the middle of the source.

7. There the writer focuses on describing the robot using long sentences. These portray it as a terrifying monster, *so we are intrigued to see if it can be defeated, or whether it will instead kill the warriors.*

8. The source is written in the third person *which creates a sense of mystery and tension.*

9. The end of the source describes the disabling of the robot, but leaves it unclear as to whether it is destroyed. *This fully engages the reader and encourages us to find out the ending.*

10. The ending is written with a mixture of long and short sentences. The short sentences *build tension, while the long sentences describe the scene.*

6 marks

My Commentary

a) The student has written 10 points, easily enough to score all 8 marks.
b) However, the student is not sure what to write, so many of the points are 'pretend' points about the effect of the reader.
c) Can you spot which one is a 'pretend' effect on the reader? (By this I mean the student is making up an effect that really isn't there).
d) Point 5 – any setting can be used to create a sense of mystery and tension. A jungle scene might be rich and wonderful, without mystery and tension at all. So this is a pretend effect on the reader.
e) Point 6 has no effect of this contrast, so doesn't include an effect on the reader.

f) Point 8 – there is only one way that writing in the third person creates more tension than writing in the first person. First person narrators can't die. This would be very relevant here, but the student doesn't say this. This is also probably irrelevant to a question on structure. It would be much easier to write that *'the focus on Eugene' fear invites us to wonder if any of the warriors will survive'*. It's the same point, but written about the structure of the text. The word 'focus' will always help you do this.

g) Point 10 simply repeats what has already been said about long descriptions in points 2 and 7. Short sentences do normally build tension (but they don't have to). If the student had quoted one and said how the focus of this particular sentence built tension, then it would gain a mark.

h) So, the answer scores 6 marks.

Response 7

1. The writer begins by focusing on the jungle and setting, especially the soft murmuring sounds. Then there is a sudden switch of focus with a single word sentence, "Ominous". *This transforms the mood and engages our attention.*

2. The next focus in on the thunderclap which introduces the Robot. *The focus has shifted from peaceful, to sudden silence to the Robot in order to build towards a climax.*

3. The next focus is on the monstrous robot. The writer gives a detailed description of the robot's legs.

4. The focus moves from body part to body part. Each of these portray the robot as increasingly terrifying and unbeatable, *which makes us fear than the warriors won't be able to kill it and instead may be killed.*

5. This focus on body parts, moving from the robot's feet to its head in rapid snapshots, *helps us see the monster from the perspective on one of the warriors and helps us understand their panic.*

6. The descriptions are bunched together as though they are thoughts crowding the warriors' minds, *revealing their terror.*

7. After these detailed descriptions of the Robot, the writer uses shorter paragraphs to focus on the final conflict with the robot.

8. The first focus of this conflict is the machine making a gigantic lunge and clearing a hundred yards in six seconds.

9. Now the focus switches suddenly on to the guns. Their bullets have no effect on the robot. *This reveals that the robot is dominant and suggests it will easily kill the warriors.*

10. The ending focuses on the robot leaning down while the bullets have no effect on it. *We imagine that the men will soon be killed.*

11. However, the final focus reveals that the Robot is disabled and falls. *The description reminds us that this condition might not be permanent and it could be powerful enough to recover.*

8 marks

My Commentary

a. The student has made 11 points.
b. As you can see, points 3, 7, and 8 do not give an effect on the reader, so they score no marks on their own. (Points 7 and 8 are really very long introductions to point 9).
c. The remaining 8 points all explain the effect on the reader, so the student gets 8 marks.

Response 8

1. The source opens with a cinematic focus on the jungle, which "was expansive…was overwhelming". *This visual description helps us picture the scene and the setting in time.*

2. Next, the focus is on descriptions of the Robot, which is a "a massive, malignant deity", made of "armour, spikes and rippling pistons" and "It soared forty feet over the treeline". *These draw the reader into the scene and help us picture the creature.*

3. Then the writer focuses on dialogue which details the conflict between Tarquin and Eugene about the plan to kill the Robot. *This creates and adds to the sense of tension.*

4. The focus at the end of the text is on destroying the robot. There is a long description as "the robot gyrated" and ending with the possibility that it might "laser" the men "like a cancer". Instead the robot is defeated and "like the Titanic, like Atlantis, the Robot tipped and sank". *This focus is dramatic and increases our sense of fear right to the very end.*

4 marks

My Commentary

a. This is a good student who clearly writes well for literature.
b. By this I mean that they realise that they need to quote as evidence. However, they have wasted time with too many quotations. Remember, you only need enough of a quotation to make a point about the *structure*.
c. However, each point is a change of focus and explains the effect on the reader, so each point gains a mark.

Printed in Great Britain
by Amazon